First US edition 2024
First published by Walker Books Ltd. (UK) 2024

Library of Congress Catalog Card Number pending
ISBN 978-1-5362-3569-2

24 25 26 27 28 29 APS 10 9 8 7 6 5 4 3 2 1

Printed in Humen, Dongguan, China

This book was typeset in Bookman Old Style.
The illustrations were done in watercolor and gouache.

Candlewick Press
99 Dover Street
Somerville, Massachusetts 02144

www.candlewick.com

ANTHONY BROWNE

Big Gorilla

A Book of Opposites

CANDLEWICK PRESS

What's the opposite of old?

Young.

What's the opposite of sad?

Happy.

What's the opposite of heavy?

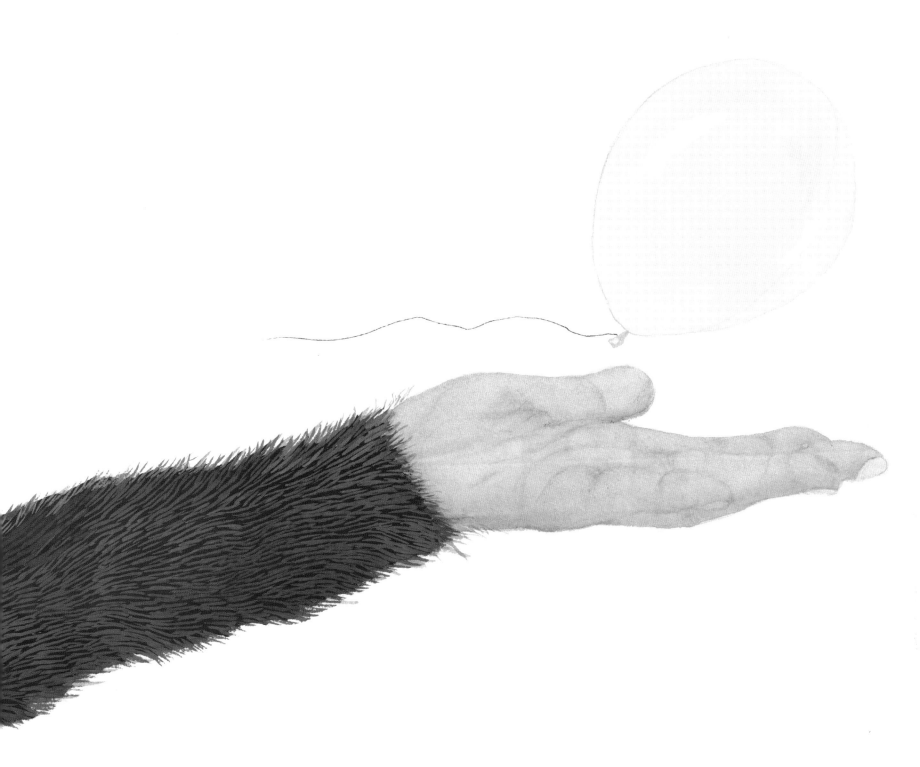

Light.

What's the opposite of alone?

Together.

What's the
opposite of
BIG?

Small.

What's the opposite of **opposite?**

The
same!